HOW TO HOUSEBREAK YOUR PUPPY AND ADULT DOG

Essentials in Puppy Training Your Dogs in Just 7 Days or Less

JAMES KRAMMER

Table of Contents

Page Intentionally left blank

Introduction

Introducing a new dog into your home is an enormous responsibility. The amount of work it takes to housetrain a dog can be overwhelming especially if you do not have a game plan going into it. This book is going to help you develop that detailed plan. While everyone's lifestyle is different and every dog is different this book is designed to fit all dogs and people, regardless of whether you are raising a working line dog for sport work or a family pet.

This is a good read for new dog owners. While the emphasis of this book is on house breaking, I have added several management techniques that you can implement to help develop a well-balanced dog who behaves in your home.

The book is going to focus on puppies, however, the contents in this book can be applied to any dog that you bring into a new home/environment. If you recently adopted a 3 year old adult dog and would like to learn how to introduce them into your home this book will work for you excellently.

House Training

House training your puppy is about consistency, patience, and positive reinforcement. The goal is to instill good habits and build a loving bond with your pet.

It typically takes 4-6 months for a puppy to be fully house trained, but some puppies may take up to a year. Size can be a predictor. For instance, smaller breeds have smaller bladders and higher metabolisms and require more frequent trips outside. Your puppy's previous living conditions are another predictor. You may find that you need to help your puppy break old habits in order to establish more desirable ones.

And while you're training, don't worry if there are setbacks. As long as you continue a management program that includes taking your puppy out at the first sign they need to go and offering them rewards, they'll learn.

When to Begin House Training Puppy

Recommendations are that you begin house training your puppy when they are between 12 weeks and 16 weeks old. At that point, they have enough control of their bladder and bowel movements to learn to hold it.

If your puppy is older than 12 weeks when you bring them home and have been eliminating in a cage (and possibly eating their waste), house training may take longer. You will have to reshape the dog's behavior with encouragement and reward.

Steps for Housetraining Your Puppy

Confine the puppy to a defined space, whether that means in a crate, in a room, or on a leash. As your puppy learns that they need to go outside to do their business, you can gradually give them more freedom to roam about the house.

When you start to house train, follow these steps:

- Keep the puppy on a regular feeding schedule and take away their food between meals.
- Take the puppy out to eliminate first thing in the morning and then once every 30 minutes to an hour. Also, always take them outside after meals or when they wake from a nap. Make sure they goe out last thing at night and before they are left alone.
- Take the puppy to the same spot each time to do their business. Their scent will prompt them to go.
- Stay with them outside, at least until they are house trained.

- When your puppy eliminates outside, praise them or give a treat. A walk around the neighborhood is a nice reward.

Housetraining with a Crate

A crate can be a good idea for house training your puppy, at least in the short term. It will allow you to keep an eye on them for signs they need to go and teach them to hold it until you open the crate and let them outside.

Here are a few guidelines for using a crate:

- Make sure it is large enough for the puppy to stand, turn around, and lie down, but not big enough for them to use a corner as a bathroom.

- If you are using the crate for more than two hours at a time, make sure the puppy has fresh water, preferably in a dispenser you can attach to the crate.

- If you can't be home during the house training period, make sure somebody else gives them a break in the middle of the day for the first 8 months.

- Don't use a crate if your puppy is eliminating in it. Eliminating in the crate could have several meanings: they may have brought bad habits from the shelter or pet store where they lived before; they may not be getting outside enough; the crate may be too big; or they may be too young to hold it in.

Signs That Your Puppy Needs to Eliminate

Whining, circling, sniffing, barking, or, if your puppy is unconfined, barking or scratching at the door, are all signs they need to go. Take them out right away.

Difficulties involved in Housetraining

Accidents are common in puppies up to a year old. The reasons for accidents range from incomplete house training to a change in the puppy's environment.

When your puppy does have an accident, keep on training. Then if it still doesn't seem to be working, consult a veterinarian to rule out a medical issue.

Do's and Don'ts in Potty Training Your Puppy

Keep the following do's and don'ts in mind while housetraining your puppy:

- Punishing your puppy for having an accident is a definite no-no. It teaches your puppy to fear you.
- If you catch your puppy in the act, clap loudly so they know they have done something unacceptable. Then take them outside by calling them or taking them gently by the collar. When they are finished, praise them or give them a small treat.
- If you found the evidence but didn't see the act, don't react angrily by yelling or rubbing their nose in it. Puppies aren't intellectually capable of connecting your anger with their accident.
- Staying outside longer with your puppy may help to curb accidents. They may need the extra time to explore.

- Clean up accidents with an enzymatic cleanser rather than an ammonia-based cleaner to minimize odors that might attract the puppy back to the same spot.

CHAPTER 2

Housetraining Tips

House-training your dog or puppy requires patience, commitment and lots of consistency. Accidents are part of the process, but if you follow these basic house-training guidelines, you can get the newest member of your family on the right track in a few weeks' time.

Establish a routine

Like babies, puppies do best on a regular schedule. The schedule teaches them that there are times to eat, times to play and times to do their business. Generally speaking, a puppy can control their bladder one hour for every month of age. So if your puppy is two months old, they can hold it for about two hours. Don't go longer than this between bathroom breaks or they're guaranteed to have an accident.

Take your puppy outside frequently—at least every two hours—and immediately after they wake up, during and after playing, and after eating or drinking.

Pick a bathroom spot outside, and always take your puppy (on a leash) to that spot. While your puppy is relieving themselves, use a specific word or phrase that you can eventually use before they go to remind them what to do. Take them out for a longer walk or some playtime only after they have eliminated.

Reward your puppy every time they eliminate outdoors. Praise or give treats—but remember to do so immediately after they've finished, not after they come back inside. This step is vital, because rewarding your dog for going outdoors is the only way to teach what's expected of them. Before rewarding, be sure they're finished. Puppies are easily distracted and if you praise too soon, they may forget to finish until they're back in the house.

Put your puppy on a regular feeding schedule. What goes into a puppy on a schedule comes out of a puppy on a schedule. Depending on their age, puppies usually need to be fed three or four times a day. Feeding your puppy at the same times each day will make it more likely that they'll eliminate at consistent times as well, making house-training easier for both of you.

Pick up your puppy's water dish about two and a half hours before bedtime to reduce the likelihood that they'll need to relieve themselves during the night. Most puppies can sleep for approximately seven hours without needing a bathroom break. If your puppy does wake you up in the night, don't make a big deal of it; otherwise they will think it is time to play and won't want to go back to sleep. Turn on as few lights as possible, don't talk to or play with your puppy, take them out and then return them to bed.

Supervise your puppy

Don't give your puppy an opportunity to soil in the house; keep an eye on them whenever they're indoors.

Tether your puppy to you or a nearby piece of furniture with a six-foot leash if you are not actively training or playing. Watch for signs that your puppy needs to go out. Some signs are obvious, such as barking or scratching at the door, squatting, restlessness, sniffing around or circling. When you see these signs, immediately grab the leash and take them outside to their bathroom spot. If they eliminate, praise them and reward with a treat.

Keep your puppy on leash in the yard. During the house-training process, your yard should be treated like any other room in your house. Give your puppy some freedom in the house and yard only after they become reliably house-trained.

When you can't supervise, confine

When you're unable to watch your puppy at all times, restrict them to an area small enough that they won't want to eliminate there.

- The space should be just big enough to comfortably stand, lie down and turn around. You can use a portion of a bathroom or laundry room blocked off with baby gates.

- Or you may want to crate train your puppy. (Be sure to learn how to use a crate humanely as a method of confinement.) If your puppy has spent several hours in confinement, you'll need to take them directly to their bathroom spot as soon as you return.

Mistakes happen

Expect your puppy to have a few accidents in the house—it's a normal part of housetraining. Here's what to do when that happens:

- Interrupt your puppy when you catch them in the act.

- Make a startling noise (be careful not to scare them) or say "OUTSIDE!" and immediately take them to their bathroom spot. Praise your pup and give a treat if they finish there.

- Don't punish your puppy for eliminating in the house. If you find a soiled area, it's too late to administer a correction. Just clean it up. Rubbing your puppy's nose in it, taking them to the spot and scolding them or any other punishment will only make them afraid of you or afraid to eliminate in your presence. Punishment will often do more harm than good.

- Clean the soiled area thoroughly. Puppies are highly motivated to continue soiling in areas that smell like urine or feces.

- It's extremely important that you use these supervision and confinement procedures to minimize the number of accidents. If you allow your puppy to eliminate frequently in the house, they'll get confused about where they're supposed to go, which will prolong the housetraining process.

Make plans for when you're away

If you have to be away from home more than four or five hours a day, this may not be the best time for you to get a puppy. Instead, you may want to consider an older dog who can wait for your return. If you already have a puppy and must be away for long periods of time, you'll need to:

- Arrange for someone, such as a responsible neighbor or a professional pet sitter, to take them for bathroom breaks.

- Alternatively, train them to eliminate in a specific place indoors. Be aware, however, that doing this can prolong the process of housetraining. Teaching your puppy to eliminate on newspaper may create a life-long surface preference, meaning that even as an adult they may eliminate on any newspaper lying around the living room.

- If you plan to paper-train, confine them to an area with enough room for a sleeping space, a playing space and a separate place to eliminate. In the designated elimination area, use either newspapers (cover the area with several layers of newspaper) or a sod box. To make a sod box, place sod in a container such as a child's small, plastic swimming pool. You can also find dog-litter products at a pet supply store.

- If you have to clean up an accident outside the designated elimination area, put the soiled rags or paper towels inside it afterward to help your puppy recognize the scented area as the place where they are supposed to eliminate.

CHAPTER 3

Training Your Puppy to Go on Potty Pads

Potty training a new puppy can be difficult if you don't know what to do, but there are several aids you can use to help your puppy go potty where you want it to go. Using potty pads (also called puppy pads, or pee pads) is one way to help teach your puppy where it is appropriate to use the bathroom. Consistency is key to this training technique, which you can then use to also teach your puppy to eventually potty outside.

Choosing a Potty Pad

The idea behind using a potty pad is to provide a visible, consistent area for your puppy to go potty. You'll want to choose something that is absorbent, easy to clean up, and large enough for the messes that your specific puppy makes. Large breed dogs may need heavy duty options compared to toy breeds. Newspapers, paper towels, cloth towels, and store-bought pee pads or indoor/outdoor carpet potty stations are all options.

Newspaper and paper towels can be messy and difficult to clean up after your puppy potties on them, but they are inexpensive. Cloth towels are absorbent but will need to be washed regularly, and your puppy is more likely to try to chew on it like a blanket or toy. Store bought pee pads are the most popular option due to their absorbency, size options, and ease-of-disposal. If you plan to train your small dog to use the potty indoors, then indoor/outdoor carpet potty stations specifically designed for dogs are good options.

Introduce Your Puppy to the Potty Pads

Allow your puppy to see and sniff the potty pads you chose. This will help it get used to the new item so it isn't scared of it at potty time. Let your puppy walk on the pad while you repeat a consistent command that you plan to say at potty time, such as "go potty."

Anticipate When Your Puppy Will Potty

While potty training your puppy, you'll need to keep them close by so that you can anticipate when they are about to go potty. There are a few key times and behaviors to watch for that will help you anticipate your puppy having to urinate or defecate:

- Puppies usually potty after sleeping, eating, drinking, and after playing. After your puppy does one of these things, you'll want to pick it up about 15 minutes later and place it onto the potty pad in anticipation of it having to urinate or defecate.
- If your puppy starts sniffing around on the ground instead of playing or chewing on a toy, this is a good indication that it needs to go potty. You'll want to pick it up and place it on the potty pad if it starts doing this.
- Your puppy may have to go potty every two to three hours. Get in the habit of taking your puppy to the potty pad every few hours.

Reward Your Puppy

Praise and treats work wonders with puppies. If your puppy goes potty on its potty pad, make sure you immediately praise it. This can be verbal in an excited tone of voice, by petting your puppy, or by giving it a special, soft treat reserved only for potty time.

Be Consistent

Keep your puppy on a regular schedule. This will make it easier for you to anticipate when your puppy may need to potty.

Say the same command phrase each time

Keep the potty pad in the same place until your puppy starts going to the potty pad by itself. Once your puppy knows what to do on the potty pad, you can slowly move it closer to the door or outside where you want your puppy to eventually use the bathroom without the use of the potty pad.

Training Mistakes to Avoid

1. Do not encourage your puppy to pull or chew on the potty pad, eat food on it, or play on it. This may

confuse your puppy as to what the purpose of the potty pad is.

2. Do not move the potty pad around until your puppy knows what it is for and is going potty on it consistently.

3. Be sure to find and use a treat that your puppy is really excited about getting. This will help with the training process.

Problems and Proofing Behavior

If your puppy isn't making it to the potty pad on time, try putting it closer to where it usually plays or eats, and then slowly move it closer to the door if you aim to eventually teach it to potty outside.

If you are having issues keeping an eye on your puppy and it has accidents when you aren't looking, try the following strategies:

- Add a bell to its collar to help you hear where it is.

- Leave the leash on for the puppy to drag behind it, which will leave somewhat of a trail for you to follow.

- Consider putting your puppy in a crate or exercise pen to nap, which may encourage it to whine if it has to potty since dogs don't like to mess where they also sleep.

If your puppy seems to be constantly urinating, talk to your veterinarian about potential problems that some puppies are known for having.

CHAPTER 4

Housetraining in 5 days using a Cardboard Box

Housetraining is easy and should not be one of those behaviors that tests your patience. Dogs are naturally clean animals and do not want to pee and poop where they sleep, so with very little effort, you can teach them that the house is sacred.

The method I am going to explain takes about five days. In some cases, it might take a little less, but it rarely takes more.

If you get your puppy on a Friday night, you can teach him on Saturday and Sunday, but you must be willing to take off work the next week to continue training.

If you are not willing to take off work the next week for the sake of your puppy, you will probably spend weeks dealing with this issue. Remember your choice when you are cleaning up puddles for several weeks after bringing your puppy home.

Invest a little time now as your new puppy is worth it.

Five Days to Housetrain Your Puppy

This method only works if the puppy is going to share your house, and will only work if the puppy is going to sleep next to you at night.

If you want to let your dog be a part of your family and sleep in your bedroom, the first thing you need is a cardboard box. The cardboard box takes the place of the whelping pen where your puppy was raised. It will keep him confined to a small area while you are sleeping or not able to watch him.

The box should be big enough for the puppy to stretch out and sleep but not so large that he can move away from any mess he makes. It should be tall enough so that he cannot climb out.

You can purchase and use a commercial crate if you want, but the main problem with crates is that dog owners will feel that they have to continue using their investment for a long time. Long term use of a crate is fine if you want to incarcerate your dog up and cause him to develop psychological abnormalities. I do not want my dogs to be afraid and run to a crate every time a strange noise scares them or a visitor comes over—there are enough neurotic dogs out there already.

A cardboard box is free and as soon as the housetraining is finished it can be broken down and tossed in the recycling bin.

A dog should never be an impulse purchase. Only bring your puppy home when the cardboard box is ready and you have time to spend on housetraining.

The First Evening With Your New Puppy

Do not give your puppy anything to drink after about six in the evening. If you arrive home after that, do not give him anything at all in the evening. Do not worry, he is not going to starve or die of thirst.

If you are bringing home a tiny Chihuahua, Yorkie, or Maltese, you can give him a little Nutrical just to keep his blood sugar up during the evening—you can order the product from Amazon or find it in most large pet stores.

Play with him outside, but do not overwhelm him, then take him for a final walk at about 11 pm before you go to bed. Do this even if you have to wake the puppy up to go outside. If you do not take him for that final walk, he will probably need to urinate in the middle of the night.

When it is bedtime, I put the exhausted puppy next to my bed and hang my hand over the side while he is falling asleep in her cardboard box. If he wakes up, the puppy can smell and touch my hand and is not going to be frightened of being alone.

You will also be bonding with the scared little puppy, so deal with the discomfort for a few nights.

A Typical Housetraining Day

5 a.m.: As soon as your puppy wakes up, take him outside or to his pads. Do not put him down until he is at the appropriate place.

Breakfast: Give him his diet, let him play with one of his toys, or play with him in the yard. When the puppy is tired he can be taken back to his box, but bring it out of the bedroom and keep it next to you.

Late morning: When the puppy wakes up, take him for a potty break before bringing him in for a light meal. Some puppies will need to urinate and defecate almost immediately, some will want to play first, or you can take him for another short walk to stimulate his bowels. When he is tired let him take another nap in his box.

Afternoon: As soon as your puppy is awake, take him out to potty. I try to give my puppy the largest meal at this time, and plenty of playtime after.

About 6 p.m.: Give the last meal of the day, take away the water, and after your puppy has had time to play carry him go to his cardboard box to sleep. The box needs to be where you are for the evening—in the living room watching TV, in the office on the internet, etc.

11 p.m.: Take the puppy for a potty break and walk, even if you have to wake him up to do so.

11-5: Most puppies will be able to sleep through the night if taken for that last potty break. Some small dogs are more likely to wake up in the middle of the night.

Saturday

Your puppy will probably wake you up early, maybe as soon as the sun is up at 5 a.m. He might whine to wake you up, he might lick your hand if it is still in his box.

Do not ignore him. He does not have a "snooze" button and this is not the time to catch a few minutes of extra sleep. If your puppy is forced to sit in his cardboard box and urinate where he sleeps, you will be setting yourself up for a lot of extra work.

Rub the sleep out of your eyes and take your puppy out to go pee. He might need to go as soon as you put him down, so lift him up and carry him outside (or to the area of the apartment you are going to use the wee-wee pads).

After your puppy has urinated, you can play with him for a while. I prefer to awake from my stupor and play with the puppy for about 20 minutes outside, since many puppies will have to go again after a short playtime.

If you want to catch another short nap before beginning your day, you can take the puppy back to his box and set your alarm for another hour. If you are ready to begin your day, go ahead and give him his breakfast and some water.

Bring the cardboard box into the living room or kitchen and when the puppy is finished eating let him take another nap. If he is not ready just after eating, play with him and he soon will be.

After about two hours, you need to wake your puppy up and take him outside or to his wee-wee pads.

If the puppy does not want to urinate right away, do not give up and let him run around the house. Stick with it.

After the puppy goes potty, praise him excessively; this is a good time to take your puppy for a walk. Tired puppies like to get plenty of sleep.

Around 11 in the morning, I give my puppy his second meal. He is already tired after his walk, so a full belly and a tired puppy equal another nap. (If not, take him for another short walk. Do not overdo it, since if you walk too far you might end up carrying him back!). Leave him in his cardboard box until after your lunch, but then take him out again before he asks to get up.

I usually give a second snack with his regular meal around three or four, and then the final light meal of the day at about six. When your puppy has eaten that final meal, take away the water.

Take him for another short walk around the yard or up and down the stairs of the apartment, then let him sleep in the box while you are watching TV. Sorry, this is one weekend you cannot go out and leave the puppy alone. Remember, if you ignore your puppy this weekend you are going to be dealing with the consequences for a long time to come.

Even if your puppy sleeps through the evening, you still need to take him for a little potty walk about 11 p.m. Since you probably woke him up to do so, he will be wide awake and want to play with you or one of his toys as soon as he has done his "business." Give him some time, but do not take him back to his cardboard box until he has peed and is ready to sleep again.

He should sleep the night through but make sure you are sleeping as close to him as possible. Try to hang your hand over the edge of the bed and into his box. If he does wake up, he will appreciate the comfort.

Small puppies learn to hold their bladders easily and are able to be housetrained by the time you bring them home.

The Other Days

Sunday

If your puppy does not wake you up at 5 am, make sure you have your alarm set and take him out for a potty break as early as the sun is up. Remember, do not put him down until he is outside or on top of his wee wee pads.

The rest of the day can go on pretty much like Saturday. Are you used to attending church on Sunday? Sorry, this is one weekend that you will have to forget about it. Concentrate on your project!

Spend the day at home, catch up on your TV shows or look at your favorite sites on the internet. Lunch, the afternoon meal, and the evening snack should all be the same time as Saturday.

Do not forget about taking him out for his evening potty break about 11. Wake him up if you need to.

Monday

By the third morning, your puppy is getting into your routine. Do not think about breaking it. You will still be home with him, so make sure he has his meals on time, his bathroom breaks on schedule, and lots of attention.

When he goes to sleep in the evening, be sure to wake him up for his 11 p.m. break.

Tuesday

This is just another day of waking at 5, feeding on schedule, plenty of naps, and a late evening potty break.

Wednesday

Is it getting tedious yet? Getting up early is no fun, but then again cleaning up accidents on the carpet for weeks to come will be even less of a joy. Spend the day caring for your new puppy.

Thursday

After your morning routine, you can leave the puppy alone today in a puppy pen. The pen is not to keep him from urinating in your house—all puppies like to explore and chew and if you leave anything down on his level he will find it and might chew it up.

Do not leave him alone for a long time. I would not plan on being away more than 3 hours. Make sure he has something to chew on and a soft blanket to lie down on.

You certainly do not need to leave food down for your puppy. Water is debatable. If you are going to be gone for 3 hours your puppy will be fine without water.

If you are leaving water down because the puppy will be alone all day, you have another problem. Your puppy will probably pee in his pen and this whole process will need to be started again. It will not go as easily the second time.

Sometime during the day, you can cut away the front of the box and keep using it as a bed for a few days. Most puppies will sleep in it during the evening and not get up in the morning until you take them out.

If your puppy still has any accidents in the house, just take a deep breath and get over it.

Having an open door makes housetraining go easier; having an older dog to teach right from wrong makes things that much smoother.

This method will work with most breeds and almost new members of your household. Puppies from pet shops or internet puppy wholesalers that come from puppy mills were probably raised in cages filthy with their own pee and poo. They have to learn to be clean, and may never be housetrained, so take a little extra time to look around and buy from a responsible breeder.

Not all puppies are able to hold their bladders by seven weeks, but most are. By the time you bring your new puppy home at eight weeks, he should not urinate in the house.

This does not mean there will never be an accident. Sometimes a puppy will be playing with kids or his toys and just cannot hold it. He will squat and urinate where he stands. It is really not his fault—anyone who has raised a toddler knows that those accidents happen even after potty training.

Do not punish your puppy for that accident. Never hit him. You can housetrain him in 5 days, just be prepared for an occasional mistake. Smile and give your puppy a scritch behind the ear.

5 Key Concepts on Housebreaking your Puppy

The first thing on any new puppy owner's mind is housebreaking. I recommend you switch the word 'breaking' for the word 'training'. I will, however, sometimes use it in my writing as I have been doing because that is what people are accustomed to saying. Doesn't 'breaking' lead you to think of doing something to your puppy to teach him? The word 'training' reminds you that this is a learning process for you and your puppy. There are five key concepts to teach your puppy:

1. Teach him where you want him to go potty

2. Teach him where you do not want him to go potty

3. Teach him to 'hold it' when he does not have access to the potty area

4. Teach him how to tell you when he needs to go potty

5. Teach him a phrase or word to go potty when you need for him to

Housetraining your puppy is similar to potty training your child. If you would not do something with a child then please do not do it with your puppy! This process is easy unless you do things that make it difficult. Punishment has no place in housetraining and will make this process both more difficult and take longer.

For ease of communication, I will assume you are outdoor training your puppy. For indoor training simply substitute 'outside' for 'potty area'. I also use the male gender in my writing. This is for ease in writing and not meant to be a slight on female puppies!

Equipment

Start by gathering the correct equipment. Think for a moment about your field of expertise. Does using the proper equipment make things easier?

You will need:

- Good quality puppy food
- Buckle collar or harness
- 3-4 foot non-retractable lightweight leash
- 15-foot non-retractable cotton web long line
- A place to confine your dog = this is the largest area your puppy will keep clean and not chew up- typically a crate or exercise pen
- A place to walk your dog for outdoor training
- For indoor training either 2 dog litter boxes or 2 frames that hold wee-wee pads and a good supply of wee-wee pads
- Small easy to swallow treats
- Carpet cleaner
- A good amount of patience
- A sense of humor

Think about these things before you start:

1. Feed your puppy on a schedule. What goes in comes out! The puppy that eats all day will need to go at unpredictable times. Feeding on a schedule allows you to predict when your puppy needs to eliminate.

2. The best place for your puppy to sleep is in a small wire crate next to your bed. It is a good idea to have a larger crate in the area of your house where you spend the most time. Consider using an indoor exercise pen if you need to leave your puppy for longer then four hours.

3. Choose a keying phrase that the entire family agrees with. I use 'be quick' with my dogs. You might also say 'business', 'go potty', 'or ' water the grass'. The only rule is that you are comfortable saying the phrase in public!

The Five Concepts of Housetraining Your Puppy

Let's see the 5 concepts of housetraining your puppy. It is important to teach all five concepts to your puppy! There is no specific order to teaching these:

The first is how to teach your puppy where to go potty

Decide where her potty area is and consistently take her there. Remember to say the word 'Outside' as you go outside or 'Inside' as you go to her indoor potty area. Give your treat five seconds after she has finished going.

The second concept teaching your puppy where not to go potty

Avoid frightening and/or punishing your puppy. Redirection without fear is the fastest way to results

The third concept is how to teach your puppy to hold it

Use confinement to teach this when you cannot watch your puppy. Use your leash (safely) indoors when you can watch him.

The fourth concept is to teach your puppy how to tell you he needs to go potty

I suggest teaching him to ring a bell instead of barking, whining, or scratching the door.

The fifth concept is how to condition a keying phrase to get your puppy to feel the internal urge to go potty when you need for him to go.

You will find that all five concepts weave together as to patiently teach your puppy what you expect from him.

I do not believe that there is such a thing a partially housetrained dog. Your puppy is either housetrained or he is not. You can use these five concepts to teach a puppy or teach an older dog, as long as the dog is of sound mind and body. It is, however, much faster and easier to teach these concepts in puppyhood!

CHAPTER 6

Tips to Help You Train Your Puppy

Congratulations on your new puppy! If this is your first dog, welcome to the wonderful world of dog ownership. Puppies are a lot of fun, but they also take a lot of work as we have learnt in the previous chapters. There are many things your puppy needs to thrive; proper training is one of the most important of these.

Puppy training can seem overwhelming. There's so much for a new puppy to learn. Not to worry! These tips can help you navigate puppy training so your new pet will become a happy and healthy member of your family.

Socializing

Socializing is just what it sounds like: It's about getting your puppy out and about to experience new people, places, and situations. Puppies that are well-socialized usually become well-adjusted adults. Many of the most common behavior concerns in dogs can stem from a lack of proper early socialization, like fear, aggression, and excessive barking.

It's important to get your puppy used to a variety of people, animals, places, sights, and sounds so he will not react poorly to them as an adult. In addition, is essential that your puppy is accustomed to being handled in different ways. This will help your puppy feel more comfortable at places like the vet and groomer.

House Training

Most new puppy owners put housebreaking high on their list of priorities. After all, it's frustrating when your dog pees in the house. House training is one of the first things you will work on with your new puppy. Get your puppy off to a good start by putting him on a regular schedule. Feed him at similar times each day. Take him outside to potty everytime he eats, drinks, or wakes from a nap.

Keep in mind that punishment does not usually have the desired effect. Things like scolding or rubbing a pup's nose in his mess will only scare or confuse him. A better method of housebreaking a puppy is to reward him with praise, treats, and playtime when he relieves himself in the right spot. A crate can also be a helpful housebreaking tool.

Crate Training

A crate is used to confine a puppy when you are unable to supervise him. If your puppy is given enough time to become comfortable in his crate, it may become one of his favorite spots. Crates can help prevent your puppy from developing bad habits like inappropriate chewing or soiling.

Crates are also good tools for house training. Most dogs will not relieve themselves in the same place where they sleep. If your dog is in the crate when he isn't outside with you or under your supervision in your house, you may be able to stop or even avoid the habit of him going potty indoors.

Confinement

A puppy shouldn't be kept in his crate for more than a few hours at a time. However, he should not have the full run of the house, even when you are home to supervise him. There are too many things in a house for a puppy to chew on, hide under, or get harmed by. Confining him to a kitchen or another small room with a door or baby gate can go a long way in preventing your puppy from developing bad habits.

Remember, a puppy who gets the opportunity to do something he finds enjoyable, such as gnawing on your furniture, is more likely to repeat the behavior. Confinement keeps him from getting these opportunities.

Prevent Destructive Chewing

Puppies love to chew. This probably isn't news to most people, especially those with a new puppy at home.

Rather than trying to prevent a puppy from chewing, teach him which things are appropriate chew toys.

Confinement is one of the tools in your arsenal when it comes to chew-training. It allows you to prevent your puppy from having the opportunity to chew on furniture, shoes, toys, or anything else you don't want him to have.

Redirecting him to appropriate toys is another part of chew training. It's not enough to tell your dog "no" when he picks up something you don't want him to have. Instead, you need to redirect him to something he can have, like a dog chew or a Kong.

Bite Inhibition

Bite inhibition is an important part of puppy training. It involves teaching your puppy to use his teeth gently. Puppies begin to learn bite inhibition from their mothers and through interaction with littermates. Many puppies need to keep learning this once they go into a home. Begin teaching your puppy bite inhibition by allowing him to use his mouth when you are playing with him, ending the playtime if he uses his teeth too hard. Once your puppy learns that the fun stops when he bites too hard, you should begin to see him using his mouth much more gently. You may also try letting out a yelp sound to remind him to be careful.

Bite inhibition is important because it keeps you safe from those needle-like puppy teeth. It also helps prevent a serious bite from occurring when your puppy grows into adulthood. Should he ever feel the need to use his teeth to defend himself, teaching your puppy bite inhibition can mean the difference between a harmless nip and a serious bite.

Positive Reinforcement

During training, puppies respond better to positive reinforcement than punishment. Punishment may stop unwanted behavior, but it does not tell the puppy what you want him to actually do. Harsh punishments may even lead to behavior issues like fear or aggression. Positive reinforcement makes your puppy want to do more of the things you want him to do.

It's quite easy to get your puppy to repeat the behaviors you like by rewarding him with praise, treats, and games. Ignore or redirect your puppy when he misbehaves and reward good behavior. Soon, your puppy will be offering good behavior on a regular basis.

Prevent Behavior Problems

When you are training a puppy, you have the ability to teach him good behavior before he begins to develop some of the more common behavior problems. Start off on the right foot by providing your puppy with lots of interesting toys, exercise, and training. A puppy left to find his own source of entertainment is more likely to engage in inappropriate behaviors.

You can also use basic obedience commands to prevent common dog behavior problems. For instance, you can ask your puppy to sit rather than allowing him to jump up when you walk through the door. By teaching your puppy appropriate behaviors, you can prevent many of the most common behavior problems.

Basic Obedience

Puppies are able to start working on basic obedience as soon as you bring them home. Training cues and commands help provide a much-needed sense of structure and set of rules for your puppy.

Use positive reinforcement to start working on basic dog training commands, and soon your puppy will be able to sit, lie down, and come on command. These basic commands will go a long way in helping your puppy grow into a well-behaved adult dog.

Puppy Kindergarten

Puppy kindergarten is a name sometimes given to dog training classes designed specifically for puppies. One of the best ways to work on all aspects of puppy training is in a puppy training class. These classes usually offer a little of everything discussed here: socialization, housebreaking, basic obedience, preventing problem behavior, and more. Best of all, it's done under the supervision of an experienced dog trainer so you have less worry about your puppy having a negative experience during training.

CHAPTER 7

Effective Housebreaking Process

Once we brought a puppy home, we look forward to years full of love, fun, and affection, but nothing beats the first few days.

As we get to know our new puppy member, we expect stressful days along the way, and one of these is a lack of effective housebreaking where you discover unpleasant things. And this is where proper potty training is essential to potty training a puppy.

A little sacrifice and dedication are needed on this matter to potty train and that the reason is simple: this is one of the things a puppy needs to learn as they get older. And it would be best to teach them first-hand.

Naturally, the mum teaches her pups where they are allowed to make a mess and where they are not. They will eventually learn through constant training and correction their mum makes.

Therefore, if you want your new puppy to be appropriately trained, you have to be consistent like a mum when training– you will be a fur mum. This action cannot be over emphasized.

This means you have to be dedicated and do things with love to avoid getting frustrated and making things difficult.

In this chapter, I have compiled all the things I think you should need to know about potty training your puppy through effective housebreaking.

So, take your puppy, and let's get started!

Potty train a puppy will state from the bare minimum ABC's of potty-training to the effective use of tools like treats and rewards, crates, puppy pads, and more. Everything you have to know in one comprehensive-effective housebreaking bible for puppies.

Basics of Potty Training Puppy Guide

To begin training your puppy for effective potty train housebreaking, it is recommended to wait until the pup is eight (8) weeks old. It would be best to follow these keys to teach your puppy before starting formal training lessons:

Be Patient

Each dog is unique and can only learn at its own pace. Some dogs learn quickly, and others take more time. Patience is indeed a virtue when it comes to effective housebreaking.

Be Kind

This goes hand-in-paw with "Be patient." Don't lose your temper if your dog doesn't "get it" right away, or appears to be ignoring you. Please do not punish your dog for not learning quickly enough. Don't punish your dog at all.

Be Flexible

If your dog is struggling to learn, be willing to change your training routine. The location may be too distracting, the time of day may be too close, or far from feeding time, the length of your training sessions for housebreaking may be too long or too short, the training exercises may need to be broken down into smaller and simpler steps. Always remember, each dog is unique. Be flexible and willing to do whatever you can to help your dog succeed.

Be Generous

Being generous with your rewards and your time can make a difference between proper potty training and excellent training with effective housebreaking. Always reward your dog's correct responses generously. A hard-work deserves a generous reward. And commit ample time to your training lessons. We're all busy these days, quality time with your pup will make training lessons fun and effective. It is advisable to plot your schedule ahead of time.

Using Rewards for Proper Training

One of the biggest keys to success with potty train a puppy is rewarding your dog correctly along with positive reinforcement. This means training your puppy something they love at exactly the right moment.

It is considered one of the fastest paths to effective housebreaking when training your puppy. It would be best to figure out what kind of reward will best motivate your dog.

All dogs are unique individuals. Most dogs are motivated by food that tastes and smells good to them.

Food treats can be tiny, which is handy for keeping them in your pocket or a pouch to use during training—and it is vital to maintain your dog's caloric intake to healthy levels.

Using treats is the form of reward we will be using throughout this training. Know what treats are suitable for your dog.

Strong- smelled meat and cheese treats are picked by many, but some are made primarily of other ingredients. It is possible for your dog not to appreciate artificial ingredients.

Small morsels of cooked chicken are a popular home-made treat. But keep in mind that what motivates other dogs may not motivate yours. It would be best to experiment and find out what your pup loves to eat.

Some dogs don't like treats, and that's where we need to turn our resourcefulness mode on. In this case, owners need to figure out something else that could motivate their dog.

A couple of pats on the head is a great reward, but it could not be for your dogs. A scratch on the belly is also an excellent idea, another unique form of petting that most owners have for their pups.

It is a matter of experimenting and finding what your little pup loves. Playing is also considered a reward such as tossing a ball, playing tug-of-war, or playfully chasing your dog for a few minutes; it could be your pup's idea of heaven when training your puppy.

The Best Puppy Potty Training Reward

Training your puppy can recognize your reaction whenever you are happy, mainly when based on the voice tone. It is rewarding when we make someone happy or smile, and that's the same for them, puppy needs the same attention.

Let your dog show you what they truly love. It is commonly noticed by their reaction to the reward you offer when you pay close attention to how they respond. But, just because they accept a piece of kibble doesn't mean they love it.

Observe them when you are giving them a treat, petting, or playing with them. If they look or walk away, it could be they weren't thrilled with what you offered, but if they get excited, stay close, and begs for more, it means they love it and are willing to work to get the reward.

For initial training, we highly recommend using a food treat as a reward while training your puppy. It's the easiest to work with and gets the fastest result but make sure your dog likes it!

After you figure out the form of reward, the second key to positive reinforcement and training your puppy is timing.

This is considered critical during early training; it would be best to immediately give the bonus after your dog gets the right action.

This means that within half-a-second, your response to their correct action must be clear and instant. Being stunned and amazed when your pup did something right from the training, and it's normal.

Keep in mind giving the treat several seconds later after your puppy got it right. It would be best to get yourself ready to be overwhelmed anytime and to deliver instant gratification.

With consistency, you'll be amazed at how quickly your pup learns to potty train.

Another important thing about timing: don't make your training lessons too long. Like humans, dogs can become bored by repetition, and let's take it from the old saying that goes, "Bored students don't learn very well".

To keep training your puppy productive, don't make them outlast your dog's attention span. Each dog is different, so you'll need to be alert and notice when his attention starts wandering.

Try for a 10-minute session and see how that goes. Shorten it if necessary. Don't lengthen it to more than 15 minutes. Repeating a short session two or three times a day is advisable rather than having one long session each day.

Reinforcements for Potty Training

The instant reward you and your dog choose will be your primary positive reinforcement for potty train a puppy.

A primary reinforcer is something your dog inherently loves. In other words, they were born loving treats, tummy rubs, etc.

Another form of reward while training your puppy is a secondary reinforcer; this is something your dog must learn to love and be motivated by it. Praise is an excellent example.

Puppies are not born loving a phrase such as "Good girl!" After all, it's just noise to them. They will learn to associate that noise with love later on.

A popular form of secondary positive reinforcement is clicker training; it is a handheld device that makes a distinctive clicking sound. That sound is a substitute for verbal praise.

When used correctly, your dog will learn to associate the clicking sound with love. I prefer using verbal praise versus a clicker, simply because your voice is something you'll always have with you.

If you prefer to use a clicker, mentally substitute "click" when the lessons say verbal praise or "Good!"

Regardless of whether you use your voice or a clicker, the most effective way to train your dog is to use primary and secondary reinforcers that are consistent.

If you prefer using your voice instead of a clicker, it would be best to choose a phrase you are comfortable with, and using the same phrase consistently will help.

Dogs are dogs, and therefore words are considered noise to their ears.

They have no idea that "Good girl," Great job," Way to go Billy," or other phrases all mean that they did something right. It would be best to use the same phrase your family members use.

Using your praise phrase several times a day is advisable when training your puppy, followed by a primary reinforcer immediately, such as their favorite treats.

Do about five repetitions, two or three times a day for two days. You can also use your praise phrase when rubbing their belly when they're eating their dinner or doing something you think they love.

They will eventually learn to love secondary reinforcers when potty training, the praise phrase, and they will later have the eagerness to hear you say it.

Throughout this chapter, I'll use the example of "Good," but substitute your own secondary reinforcement choice. Remember to use it—and only it—consistently.

During early potty train, the combination of primary and secondary positive reinforcement is considered extremely powerful and useful rather than using either form of motivation alone.

Treats are not needed forever, and therefore carrying treats around in your pocket will not last long. As your dog learns, obeying becomes a habit eventually, and using treats consistently, or other primary reinforcements are somehow not needed.

But, whenever teaching your pup something new, make sure to use them consistently. Using secondary positive reinforcement continually is always a good idea. It is a way of thanking your dog for doing what you asked, and of course, simple common courtesy is rewarding.

We can guide you on when to start decreasing the use of treats or other primary positive reinforcements later on. Now that you have the basic knowledge of rewards and timings let's get the training started!

Effective Housebreaking Potty Training Breakthroughs

Effective potty train housebreaking is considered an essential element of a loving, lifelong relationship between you and your dog. If you don't teach your new best friend not to pee and poop in your house, he won't be your friend for long!

Fortunately, housetraining a puppy (or adult dog) to potty train isn't complicated with positive reinforcement. All you have to do is prevent peeing and pooping in the house, and reward peeing and pooping while you take them outside.

While putting this simple concept into practice isn't difficult, it does require your diligence, dedication, and patience. But the rewards are definitely worth the effort!

We'll provide some general information about dogs on which our effective housebreaking techniques are based, explaining the benefits of puppy pads or crate training, and the step-by-step process for housebreaking your dog.

5 Facts Before Housebreaking

Here are five facts that can guide your potty train housebreaking:

Fact 1: Adult dogs can be housebroken the same as puppies when it comes to potty training.

If you adopt an adult dog, you may not have to worry about housebreaking if they have been adequately trained. It is unnatural for a dog to know that it is not right to go indoors, even the smartest one.

They must undergo training to understand as most adult dogs did, but we can't assume right away.

Some adult dogs were kept outdoors, raised in a cage ever since they were pups, or were improperly trained by their previous owners. In this case, you will have to start fresh and do housebreaking using the same basic techniques for a puppy.

However, adult dogs don't have to go or wee as often as puppies, which makes the training a lot easier. On the other hand, adult accidents can create bigger messes, so it would be best to prepare yourself.

Fact 2: Puppies have limited bladder & bowel control.

A puppy younger than 20 weeks old has to go once every hour when awake. A very young puppy, under 12 weeks old, will need to go more often than every 30 minutes to two hours or even more frequently.

For an older puppy, a general rule for potty training and determining the number of hours they can go without doing their dog litter is to take their age in months and add one.

Therefore, a four-month-old could hold for about five hours. For small breeds, they can't keep it too long, but they can hold it a bit longer for large breeds. This is a general rule, and your puppy's control may vary. When asleep, puppies can hold even longer than they can when awake.

Fact 3: Dogs like to sleep in a clean area and not with dog litter.

Just like humans, dogs prefer to sleep in a clean area. In the wild, canines such as wolves, coyotes, and foxes rest in a den and go outside to relieve themselves.

And through this, their pups learn to do the same thing because dogs will try their best not to soil their sleeping area.

A puppy is less likely to potty in a small-so-called den, and confining them in whenever you can't keep an eye on them, can help avoid starting a bad habit of going anywhere and wee wherever they like.

Fact 4: Dogs do best when kept to a routine schedule with potty training.

Feeding your dog at a regular time will help to potty on a regular schedule.

Letting your pup eat and drink whenever they want can give you a hard time knowing when he needs to go out. Taking them out on a regular schedule is also advisable.

Fact 5: Punishing a dog after he has an accident in the house is pointless and may do more harm than good.

Your dog will not understand that you are upset about something that happened in the past—even if it was just a minute or two ago.

This could cause trauma to a pup and might have a hard time figuring out what the punishment was. And for this, they might get the wrong message far from what you want them to perceive.

Your Dog Common Scents

A dog's sense of smell is strong, and therefore they rely on the scent to look for their 'toilet'. They can recognize the same spot where they have gone potty before through scents, and by this unique smell, it gives your dog a hard time to resist as it is a sort of sign that says it is their 'toilet'.

It would be best to make sure there is no odor of urine or feces before starting to potty training a new pup.

What can I put on my carpet to stop my dog from peeing on it?

Using vinegar or ammonia as cleaning solutions is not advisable as these scents are close to the urine smell.

Using baking soda, club soda, or purchasing special odor-eliminating cleaners from a pet store is better.

When cleaning up the past mistakes your dog did you want to learn how to stop dog from peeing in same spot. Try marking the rooms with the smell of you and other family members can help your pup resist going potty in that area and not in the same area.

And this is why an untrained dog that can't go outside often runs to a rarely used area of the house to go.

If your dog ends up staining and peeing the couch cushion here are some useful tips on how to get dog pee out of the couch.

Once the scent wee and poop have removed, it would be best to spend time in every room with your dog, especially the places that are used rarely.

Playing and sitting on the floor with your dog for several minutes in each room for a couple of days, and soon enough, the room will be left with a scent that can give them a sign that it's not a potty zone for dog litter.

It might take a lot of effort to mark every area in your house this way. This method is more of a passive deterrent rather than a foolproof method to prevent your dog from going potty inside. On a side note, the action is needed, especially for a puppy. However, if all else fails and your dog continues to pee on the carpet here are some helpful tips on how to get dog pee out of carpet.

How to Crate Train Your Puppy

Take your puppy and let them have the privilege to run free around the house can sometimes bring disadvantages, and one of them is going potty anywhere and whenever they want.

Keeping an eye on them at all times to prevent them from pottying anywhere can be quite impossible.

Instead, it would be best to train them up for success instead of failure by using puppy pads or start crate training with positive reinforcement.

Remember Fact 3 in Potty Training: *Dogs Like to Sleep in a Clean Area*–by confining a pup to a "den," this, can help them from peeing or pooping since they want to keep their own space clean.

Also, doing this, helps you to predict when they need to go accurately. It usually happens the moment they are released from their crate.

Creating a cozy den for your pup out of a dog crate is recommended, and therefore picking out the best dog crate for your puppy is essential, especially when it comes to the crate size that it is big enough for them to stand, turn around, and lie comfortably. But not too big that gives them a space to make it as their toilet.

Line the crate with a towel that you've used, or a shirt that you've worn, so your scent is present.

It would be best to make the crate comfortable for your pup by placing the crate in a quiet area away from distractions, not too close to a window or in a high-traffic area of your house, and not away from the pack and your family.

Praising Your Dog Every Effort

Take your puppy and praise your dog when they go in the crate, and if they won't, put some treats on the crate entrance.

Gradually move the treats farther in until they go all the way to get them. Don't close the door yet, and let them go in and out as they please.

Putting treats on the crate entrance can help and make it a fun game by tossing treats going in few times in a row–off and on throughout the day.

Say "crate" whenever you want them inside, and praise them when they do.

After you think they are comfortable with the crate, and eagerly runs in to get the treats, close the door for a second after they go in; open it and let them out. Doing this a few times is advisable.

Close the door and leave it that way as you feed them few treats through the crate bar spaces and let them out. The next step is to stuff a hollow chew toy with something delicious.

Let your puppy sniff the stuffed chew toy and place it in the crate. Close the door with your puppy on the outside for them to beg you to open the door to let them in which usually takes a few seconds.

Use positive reinforcement and praise them for going in by saying "crate." Once they get caught up licking the chew toy, slowly walk away and return before they finish enjoying it. Open the door and don't let them take the chew toy outside of the crate, if they do, take it from them.

The next step is to tie the freshly stuffed chewing toy in the crate and leave it open. They either want themselves in or stay outside of the crate.

But, most pups prefer to be in for the chewing toy. This could make them fall asleep inside when finished, and you can then slowly close the door.

Using Crate Naps When Your Puppy Get Sleepy

When a puppy is sleepy, putting them in the crate can help. Encourage them to go in with treats by saying "crate" when you think they're about to fall asleep. You can then close the door after they go in.

If you found them already asleep, slowly pick them up and carry them as gently as you can; don't forget to close the door.

With pre-conditioning, some puppies quickly accept being confined in their crate at night, but some will whine and bark for you to let them out.

Putting a cover over the crate will help them settle down and fall asleep. But mind the temperature that it's not too hot or too cold.

It would be best to ignore their whining and barking for you to let them out. Otherwise, they will get the wrong message that it is the key to getting themselves out of the crate, which is a bad idea.

After a few minutes, pups will settle down and go to sleep. However, if they start whining after being quiet for a while, they may need to go.

They should be taken outside, but don't let them out when crying. Please wait for a little while for them to pause from whining, and quickly open the door.

Making some noise that can make them stop whining is advisable when they don't pause. Immediately take them out before they start making noise again.

Using the crate at night and during the day whenever you can't keep an eye on your puppy or have them outside. Using the crate as punishment is not advisable.

Scolding your puppy and locking them in the crate is not a good idea. They could associate the crate with punishment. We want them to think their crate as a comfortable den, and not a jail cell.

By following these helpful steps, your pup will consider the crate to be their safe-cozy den after a few days and happily do so.

How to Train Your Puppy to Use Puppy Pads

Using the best pet training pads is a great way for potty training. Puppy pee pads are also called dog pee pads.

Using this along with the playpen idea mentioned in this book, they can allow you to eventually let go of the playpen and let your puppy roam around the house while you are away without having accidents all over the place. In case it happens, we got the best tips for how to get old dog urine smell out of carpet.

This option is great for all dogs to go in one area while you're gone. Choose a suitable area inside your home where you can place the puppy pad.

When your pet starts to show signs that it needs to go, take them where the puppy pad is and encourage them by using commands such as "go pee!" and "good boy!".

If your puppy had gone potty in a different area in the house, lead your pup back to the pad—repetition is the key.

Once the pad is fully absorbed, pick the pad up by holding the four corners to conceal it, and then carefully throw the pad away. Make sure to wash your hands after. If you're looking for the best, here's a helpful guide to what you should be looking for when you're looking for the best puppy pads to buy.

When your puppy gets comfortable using training regularly, start moving the pad outside to get them used to go outside.

Do not punish your pet for accidents – this can be very frightening for them and give you huge setbacks in training the pup. A gentle voice with positive encouragement will go a long way. These are excellent ideas as you can get rid of the crate method later on.

Since the puppy has learned how to do their business on the puppy pad, they will keep this in mind, whether they are in the house. You can take them out of the crate and let the puppy have a bit more freedom while you are gone.

Simply leave the pad on a corner that's acceptable for them, and they will relieve themselves there rather than all over the house.

Successful potty training is all about timing. The goal is to have your puppy in the right place (outside) at the right time (when they need to go) and avoid having them in the wrong place (inside) at the wrong time (when they need to go). This can be easier when you're able to predict when your puppy needs to go.

Keep in mind the Fact 2: *Puppies Have Limited Bladder & Bowel Control*. Usually, puppies need to pee right after waking up from a nap and poop within a couple of minutes.

Rewarding your puppy For doing a good job is another critical element of timing; we have covered this in our Training With Basics. Your puppy goes potty when and where you prefer, your immediate and lavish rewards (praise and yummy treats) can teach them to repeat this correct behavior.

A dog that is not housebroken should be restricted to one of these three situations at all times:

1. Under your constant and attentive supervision.
2. Outside with you.
3. Confined inside the crate/den.

Situation 3 is where your puppy should spend most of the time during the housebreaking process. Did you notice that we did NOT include a situation where you leave your dog outside all the time?

Many people mistakenly think that puppies kept outside will be less trouble—after all, they won't be peeing and pooping in your house, and they won't need your constant supervision, right?

But here is the reality: puppies left outdoors and unsupervised for long periods seldom become housebroken. They tend to bark, chew, dig, and escape from your yard.

How to Teach Your Puppy to Go Potty Outdoor

Outdoor puppies also become so excited on the rare occasions when they are allowed indoors (excited puppies tend to pee without warning).

Here's how to take them outside and potty training your four-legged friend outside:

1. Determine where you want your dog to go. It's best to pick a doggy toilet area that's relatively close to the door, so you and your dog don't have to go too far to go. Give the location some thought, because after they're trained, your dog will continue to use this place as a toilet. This is convenient for clean-up time, especially if you have a large yard—and your family won't have to be wary of little "landmines" when playing outside in the non-doggy- toilet areas.

2. Know when your puppy has to go. Until your puppy is trained to give you sign which eventually will happen sooner or later, when they need to go, you have to be familiar at deducing this. Sometimes a puppy will need to go with a minute interval within

5-8 minutes. And therefore, it is best to wait for a few more minutes until they are finished.

Here's when you should take them outside:

- Immediately first thing in the morning.
- After letting them out of the crate/den.
- Every 30 to 60 minutes while they're awake, based on the age (see Fact 2).
- After eating or drinking.
- When doing something for a while (like chewing on a toy), and then gets up and starts looking around.
- Starts sniffing the floor.
- When going to an area where they've gone potty before.
- Running around and excited more than usual.
- When looking at or wandering near the door.
- When pacing, whining, or starts to squat (duh!).

Note: Male puppies squat to pee just like female puppies (versus lifting a leg) until they are 4-9 months old. Keep your puppy under your constant and attentive supervision, or confined in a crate, when indoors.

It only takes a couple of seconds for a puppy to squat and pee, so you must watch them closely. Don't stare at them, it'll make them nervous, but keep an eye when they're out of their crate.

This will be easier if you limit their movements by keeping them on a leash or restricting them to one or two rooms.

Don't think you can watch TV, wash the dishes, or do something else and keep an eye on your pet at the same time. If you become distracted or preoccupied, accidents could happen, which might make housebreaking longer, and a difficult task.

When Messy Accidents Happens

It's your responsibility to take your pet outside when they need to go. Accidents happen, and it will never be anyone's fault– hence it's called 'accident'.

Take your dog to a designated toilet area every hour or whenever they need to go *(see Step 2),* whichever is less, and teach them to go on command.

It would be best to fill your pocket with treats every hour to avoid forgetting to give them treat. After releasing your puppy from their crate, take them straight to the designated toilet area.

Encourage them to go quickly by calling "outside, outside, outside" enthusiastically. Taking your time isn't recommended as they might pee or poop en route out of excitement.

Making them hurry is also a good idea to jiggle their bowels and bladder, so the moment they are in the toilet area, they go right away. Taking your dog out every hour as possible even if they are old enough to hold longer is also a good idea.

Leading Your Pup to The Correct Place

Use a leash while potty training, even if you have a fenced yard, To lead them to the correct place. This will also get them used to go while on the leash. Stand quietly, don't stare at them, and wait until they start.

If they stare at you instead of doing their business, they smell the treats in your pocket, look away and pretend to ignore them. Eventually, they started sniffing and prepared to go.

When they start to go, say "go potty" quietly, so you don't startle them.

Choosing another cue that you are comfortable speaking in public is a good idea, and it would be best if the other family members use this word/phrase whenever pottying.

Once they had finished, give them a generous amount of tasty treats and lots of enthusiastic praise immediately–lavish rewards mean quicker results.

These steps are essential for potty training. If you only open the door and let them out by themselves to go and reward them when they come back in, the housebreaking will take longer.

Your dog would think the reward was because of coming back in rather than going potty, and you will miss the opportunity to train them to go on command.

It is advisable to spend time playing, training, and taking your puppy for a nice walk when they're old enough.

Taking them outside to potty and ignoring them after you quickly bring them in could make them think that fun ends after potty training.

Consequently, they may become reluctant to go when they are outside and end up going in when they can no longer hold it.

Praising your puppy for going potty and taking them for a walk as an extra reward for a job well done is a good idea. This additional reward will encourage them to go more quickly.

What If They Don't Go Potty When You Take Them Outside?

If your puppy enjoys the great outdoors but doesn't go within a few minutes, take them back in, put them back in the crate and try again in 10 minutes. If they only potty and have a hard time doing so in the Winter use these 4 tips on how to potty train a puppy in the winter.

Repeat the process until they go. Your puppy will learn that they need to go when they are taken outside, or they will be taken back in the crate again–no potty, no freedom.

Eventually, they will go in the appropriate place at the appropriate time and for you to be able to give the appropriate rewards.

Controlling your puppy's intake is also a good idea to know when they need to go by their age and size. Feeding your pet on a set schedule can help them potty on a regular schedule.

A puppy needs to go around 30 minutes after eating or drinking. Allowing them to eat whenever they want is not a good thing as it is unlikely to know when they need to go out.

Feeding them at the same time each day is highly recommended, and a puppy younger than three months should be fed three times a day although, older ones can be fed twice a day.

Handling Inevitable Accidents

Accidents can be avoided by following the given steps, but that doesn't mean it won't happen. When an accident happens, don't get upset.

Instead, try to determine why it happened. There could be several reasons, such as getting distracted when keeping an eye on your pup, forgetting to take them outright in time, etc.

Despite what many people believe, dogs do not get pee or poop intentionally because they are angry, lonely, or want to "get back at you" for something. Dogs don't think of pee or poop as something "nasty" to be used out of spite.

And the so-called look of "guilt" or cowering in "shame" when you scold them is actually your dog's way of showing appeasement and submitting to your obvious anger. If you do not catch your puppy in the act, do nothing (except clean it up).

Do not—repeat—do not rub his nose in it, hit, yell, shake, or punish them in any way. Dogs don't think about the time the way humans do. Your dog will not understand that you are upset about something that happened in the past—even if it was just a minute or two ago.

What If You Do Catch Him in The Act?

If you catch your dog squatting and about to go inside the house, make a sudden, surprising sound—such as slapping the wall—not to scare him, but to get the attention to momentarily stops what they're doing.

Encourage your puppy to run outside with you. "Outside, outside, outside!" And finally, reward your puppy lavishly for going potty in the right place.

In any case, be sure to clean up all accidents quickly and thoroughly. You must eliminate any lingering scent, so it doesn't invite your puppy back for a repeat performance.

How Long Before He's Housebroken?

When can you safely start leaving your puppy or dog alone in the house for a while? It depends on many things, including the age, size, and most importantly, the owner's diligence in training them.

In general, following these potty training guidelines should be making good progress within two months on your pet.

But some dogs learn quickly while others take more time. Gradually increase the amount of time you allow your puppy to be indoors, out of the crate, and monitor the progress.

Adult dogs generally need to go out at least once every four hours—first thing in the morning, around midday, late in the afternoon, and before going to sleep.

Hiring a pet sitter is advisable when you think you can't get home on time to let your puppy out often enough. Accidents and setbacks are normal. It would be best to continue following the above steps and the best key to success: patience.

Be Alert for Special Potty Training Circumstances

There are a few reasons why it might be particularly challenging to housebreak a dog.

Dogs who were raised in puppy mills or pet stores, or who were regularly confined without the opportunity to go away from their sleeping area, might take longer to housebreak and require more patience and understanding from the owner.

Sudden changes in dog food brands or overindulgence in treats or table scraps can cause diarrhea. There may be physical reasons, such as a urinary infection. Be sure to get your dog checked thoroughly by your vet.

Advanced Housebreaking Potty Training Tips

As a dog owner, you should be familiar with the clicker. A clicker is a great tool not just for house training when potty train a puppy, but also for all manners of obedience training.

It is a small-sized object that you hold in your hand to make a sharp clicking or cracking sound.

Here are some tips to help you learn how to use this tool properly:

Using a clicker with a food treat is mandatory. Press it to make a single click and, at the same time giving your pet a food treat.

Clicking alone without a treat is not enough and can disappoint you when they can't figure out what the click is for.

When it comes to house training, consistency is vital.

Using a clicker lets them know which action is being rewarded, such as pressing the clicker with a treat when they go in the designated area. They will eventually know which act is being rewarded.

Here are a few examples of when to reward your puppy using a clicker:

- When they look at you every time you call their name. This is a reward for recognizing their name. It makes it easier for you to call them.

- When sitting when you say "sit". Sometimes pups can be rowdy, and their breathing may not be able to handle all the activity. You can then teach them to sit down and relax.

- Teaching them to get "down". Clicking should be done at the precise moment their elbows hit the floor. This is another rest exercise for your pup.

- Dropping or giving an item that is in their mouth. This can even save them from distress when something is in the mouth that could choke them. It also saves you from distress when your favorite shoe is in your pet's mouth.

- Entering the crate. The use of a crate can also help them relax, and it also helps with house training.

- When stops whining or barking. This is the sort of behavior that must be discouraged. The best way to do that is not through punishment, but by rewarding the pup the moment they stop doing it.

- When they use puppy pads. Right when they use it to potty, click and reward them for proper housebreaking.

Using the clicker is not permanent. Gradually eliminate the use of it by reducing 10% of the time you click whenever your pet has done something right until it increases to 15% and so on.

Sooner or later, they go in the designated area to keep you happy and used to it. It has now become a habit and does without a clicker and treat. The clicker is also another signal of affections. It is like their favorite treat you gave when they did something right.

Clicker emphasizes what behavior is being rewarded. It allows them to focus on the particular activity that you want to be rewarded and reinforced.

Use Positive Reinforcement

Dogs are susceptible to human emotions. Shouting at your puppy is strongly discouraged. It can be quite traumatic, especially for a little pup. It only teaches them to fear you and nothing else.

Know that soiling and peeing are natural body functions, and they are not ought to associate any negative emotions with natural functions. Take the time to calm yourself instead of getting angry and, instead of shouting, speak assertively.

Through this, every time it will help them recognize that you are the authority in the pack and learn to respect your rank.

Since you have shown your pup that you don't like the mess, it would be best to clean it up and bring your pup to your chosen relieving area. Right there and there, allow your pup to pee or defecate.

Don't forget to give praise when they do–giving your puppy a treat to reinforce the idea that relieving themselves in a specific place is the right thing to do.

Housebreaking is Just a Matter of Routine

The first thing is first, observe your puppy. During the time you potty train a puppy, figure out how long it takes to digest the food and drink before they are ready to relieve themselves.

When you have used a crate, it's easy to know when they want to out when they paw around, sniff the ground, whine, and turn around a few times as if looking for something.

If these behaviors are present, take your pup out to the relieving area to potty.

For a false alarm case, you can take them back in the crate to help them remember that going out means pottying when it's crate time.

Puppies quickly catch on to the routine one way or another by being consistent and patient with the way you treat your pup.

Every successful trip outside should be celebrated by praising your dog, patting, and playing. And of course, the treat.

Other than peeing and pooping time after meal hours, note that some puppies need to go every hour or every two hours. Well, that will be the case for younger pups.

Older pups can hold on to it a lot longer and tend to be more disciplined later on.

Watch Your Energy Levels

A stressed pup can also be tough to train and control. Cesar Milan, also known as the Dog Whisperer, said that dogs are also sensitive to their owner's energy levels.

They sense when you are in a rush, nervous, and being impatient. This means you have to be mindful of your voice tone when giving commands.

Cesar says that a squeaky tone or even a loud tone of voice can stress your puppy and make housebreaking a lot more complicated than it should be.

Make Your Pup Feel Safe and Loved

A stressed pup will be challenging to train. It's important to make sure every time they feel safe in the environment, loved and cared for by the family. This can strengthen the bond between you and your pup.

The 6 Time Rule

On average, your pup needs to relieve itself at least 6 times each day. That's the average number of trips to the relieving area that you might have to make. It takes patience, but it is beneficial for you and your dog in the long run.

You can count each day how many times you have taken your pup outside, that way you can time each trip and estimate just how many trips you still need to make.

Chewing and Uncontrolled Peeing

Pups chew anything and therefore keeping important things away from their reach is necessary. Paying attention to their energy level is advisable when starting your day.

Most people show a lot of affection when they see their puppy and could be a hindrance when housebreaking them. This is not what its mom would do when raising the pup. The mummy would show calm of assertiveness, and you should too.

It is best to show affection to your pup after some exercises, and a shred of discipline has shown. Showing excitement first thing in the morning could encourage your pup to wet themselves excitedly.

There could also be a medical issue at hand when your pup peep uncontrollably. If the tip above doesn't work, it is advisable to take them to the vet to rule out any possible illness.

So, if you're housebreaking and potty train a puppy, remember they don't know anything yet, and for an adult dog, there may be some old habits to "unlearn" first.

Be patient, be consistent, and be encouraging. A few weeks of dedicated effort will result in a lifetime of clean floors and a beautiful relationship with your dog.

CHAPTER 8

How to Housebreak a Puppy or Older Dog

One of the most common questions I get every day concern problems people have with house training their dogs.

As I have stated earlier in this book, there's no such thing as an almost housebroken dog. Either he is or he isn't. Saying a dog is almost housebroke is like saying your wife is almost pregnant. When a dog is housebroken he never uses the house for his toilet.

Many people do not understand why their dog does not know what to do when taken outside. Just turning a dog out in the back yard by himself a few times a day is not the way to house train a dog.

Merely taking him outside also does not mean he knows what he's being taken outside for. The biggest problem between the dog and the owner is that the dog would love to please but he doesn't know how to communicate with you.

Housebreaking in theory is very simple. It is finding a means of preventing the puppy from doing his duties in the house and only giving him the opportunity to do it outside. It also means that the dog learns to communicate with you about going when told to go and about letting you know when he has to go outside.

A dog is a creature of habit and because he learns by association, if his training is consistent he will quickly learn there is no other place to relieve himself other than outdoors.

We take advantage of a very natural instinct of the dog - his desire to keep his sleeping quarters clean - i.e. not to mess his bed. We offer a dog a den in the form of a dog crate. This becomes his bed that he cannot get out of. If the dog crate is the right size he will not soil it. Puppies may not initially like it (some will scream their heads off) but within a few days they will accept it without a problem.

Dogs are and always have been den and pack animals. Canines naturally and instinctively prefer the shelter of a den. In the wild the young are raised in dens. They spend a great part of their first year very close to their den. In homes, dogs often choose their den. They will get under a desk, behind a couch, in a closet, etc.

A dog crate is a perfect, natural bed for the dog and a safe, natural spot to put the pet whenever necessary for the dog's safety or the owner's peace of mind.

If you are appalled by the idea of confining him to a cage, let me dispel any idea of cruelty. You are actually catering to a very natural desire on the part of the dog. In his wild state, where does a dog bed down for the night? Does he lie down in the middle of an open field where other animals can pounce on him? No! He finds a cave or trunk of a tree where he has a feeling of security - a sense of protection. The correct use of a crate merely satisfies the dog's basic need to feel safe, protected, snug and secure.

Now with this said. Some puppies will scream their living heads of - some for a couple of days when you put them in the crate. The question you need to answer is "would I rather get the dog used to the crate or would I rather clean up dog crap on my rug"? An easy question to answer.

Pups do get over the fact that screaming gets them no where - as long as you ignore it and DO NOT TAKE THEM OUT OF THE CRATE WHEN THEY ARE SCREAMING. If if bother you - put the crate in the basement or the garage or leave the house for a few hours. Trust me - it will stop when it gets tired. Those who give in create their own problems.

Small pups will naturally sleep 15 to 18 hours a day. This is normal. They quickly learn that the crate means taking a nap.

I keep a plastic bowl of all-natural dog treats near my crate. The liver biscotti that we sell are perfect. They don't smell and they don't get moldy with age. Every time I put a pup in the crate I give a "CRATE" command and toss 3 or 4 liver biscottis into the crate. It gives the pup a nice reason to go in. You will be surprised how quickly they expect to get a treat when they go into the crate. Going in becomes a positive experience.

As a dog ages and learns I will give the "CRATE" command before I toss the treats in. I will expect the dog to go in on their own because I just told them to do it. This exercise is the beginning of teaching your dog to go to his crate when people come to the house. Dogs that bark and act stupid when they hear the door bell need to be told to go to their crate. This is how that training is started.

When thinking of the size of a crate needed for your dog, think small. Think den not condo! The use of too large a crate for a puppy will encourage the pet to use a small portion of it for a bed and the remainder as a relief station!

The puppy should only be allowed to relieve itself out doors. It is OK to place the crate in the bedroom of the person who will be responsible for that early morning trip. This is a temporary situation. I am not a fan of a dog sleeping in the bedroom. It often causes adult dog to develop issues of dominance. Once the pup is old enough to sleep the night through without having to go outside I recommend that the crate be moved into another room.

A crate is never meant to be used as a place of punishment for the puppy, so a couple of safe toys would be welcome for crate-time. A kong filled with peanut butter or cream cheese goes a long way towards keeping a puppy quiet in a crate. Be careful of the toys you choose to leave - soft squeaky toys with bells are not healthy for pups. To often pups chew up these soft toys and get parts of them stuck in their bowels which often kills them.

Start crate training while you remain in the same room with the crated dog, frequently praising him and letting him know clearly it is pleasing to you that he remains in the crate, quietly. Frequent trips out of the room with quick returns with a treat through the bars will condition the dog to your comings and goings.

Gradually extend your absent periods, and in a short time, you can be gone several hours. While in the crate, the dog should not be scolded except for chewing on the wires. You can make it clear that you are not pleased with screaming but often that does not impress the pup. So, ignore it.

Crate confinement works so well that most dogs soon choose the crate for naps and, in general, consider it their own private domain. They learn that they can go into their crate and sleep and no one will step on them or jump on them.

At night take the puppy out and give him an opportunity to do his duties. If you are in a protected area (a fenced back yard) let him go free of the leash. Be sure to stay out there with him. Lavishly praise him with GOOD OUTSIDE when he has completed his duties. Take him inside at once and put him in his bed.

A puppy is NEVER ALLOWED TO HAVE FREE ACCESS TO THE HOUSE unless you have your eyes on the pup. If he poops on the floor because you turned your back for 45 seconds - well you screwed up and made a mistake. Don't blame the pup for your mistake.

The only time pups are loose is just after they come in from going outside and then only for short periods of time. All of my interaction with my pups is done outside. I NEVER leave a dog unattended and loose in the house until it is 18 to 24 months old and then only for short periods.

Pups must go out first thing in the morning (and I mean first thing) take the dog outside. He's been clean all night - and holding it all night - he will do his duty in a hurry because HE HAS TO GO. Now bring him in and give him freedom, but in the kitchen only. A child's gate at the kitchen doorway is an excellent barrier to the other rooms in the house. Give him his freedom while breakfast is being prepared and while you are eating breakfast. After your breakfast, and when you have time to take him out, feed him his breakfast - and take him out immediately. Remember the rule - outside after each meal. Dogs relieve themselves after SLEEPING - EATING AND HAVING EXERCISE.

Now bring him in and put him in his crate and go about your normal routine of the morning. He should stay in the crate until about 11:00 to 11:30 A.M. Then out of the crate and outside. Bring him in, and while you are preparing and eating lunch let him have the freedom of the kitchen but only when you have "eyes on the dog."

At dinner time as soon as he has finished his last mouthful - take him outside. After he has completed his duties, bring him in and again give him the freedom of the kitchen while you are preparing dinner and during the dinner hour. Give him another trip outside about 8:00 P.M. - and again just before your bedtime. Some pups need to be exercised more than others to get them to relieve themselves. Exercise always increases the urge to pee or poop.

The bottom line is you cannot take your dog outside too much. If you take him out every hour then he learns that he is going to have a chance to go outside to do his business. So when someone tells you to wait for 4 hours - I would ask WHY if you can take him out more often? Why wait that long if you are home. We want to establish a pattern and what better way than to take the dog out all the time. Also do not underestimate how important it is to ask your pup if he WANTS TO GO OUTSIDE just before going out and praising GOOD OUTSIDE WHEN HE DOES GO. I tell my adult dogs GOOD OUTSIDE.

One last point on your dogs house breaking. A commercial kibble diet takes 14 to 15 hours to go through the dog. An all-natural diet goes through the dog in 5 to 6 hours. I strongly recommend that you consider doing your research on all-natural diets.

A couple of points on how to house train your dog:

1. Do not vary your dog's diet.
2. Treats should be given as a reward for the puppy going into the crate.
3. Bring him in as soon as he does his business.
4. Praise every time you see him pee or poop. Do this forever. Reinforcing good behavior never hurt anything.
5. Dogs who go out and just dink around and then go in their crate need more exercises when they go outside. A long walk will often cure the problem. BE SURE TO PRAISE WITH GOOD OUTSIDE or whatever

you want - then when you have the dog in the house and say "DO YOU WANT TO GO OUTSIDE" he will learn what you mean.

6. Older dogs are house trained exactly like young pups.

Paper Training

Let me say a few words about "paper breaking," or should I say against it. As I said before, a dog learns by association and if you allow him to do his duties in the house on paper you are telling him in effect that it is all right to do it within the four walls of the house - you are making this association in his mind - so later when you expect him to do his duties outside, he may think you are a little crazy and you can't blame him.

Any healthy pup 8 weeks of age or older, even in cold weather, can go outside. Of course you don't leave him out long enough to get chilled. You take him out just long enough to do his duties.

With all of this said there is always the occasional pup who will pee and poop in the crate. No matter how often you take him outside. This usually happens because of the living conditions the dog has before you got it. If the litter was not kept clean then the pup has learned to be a pig. All you can do is continue on - its a pain to clean the crate and the dog. But eventually they will catch on.

Unfortunately most of these dogs never get that chance because they seal their fate by their unclean actions. I recently had a friend who raised her own litter and the pups were kept impeccably clean. One male she kept took 6 months before he would stop peeing in the crate at night. She got up in the middle of the night for months before the problem went away. So the moral of the story is that you need to do EVERYTHING right and even then things can go wrong. We are dealing with animals and sometimes they defy our good sense.

With a little effort on your part and the use of this method the puppy can be housebroken very quickly. But remember there is more than peeing and pooping in the house that goes along with housebreaking.

Allowing a dog to be loose when you are gone is a little crazy unless you are 100% sure the dog will not chew your walls, your shoes, your furniture or anything else it takes a liking to. SO, KEEP YOUR DOGS IN DOG CRATES until they are 18 to 24 months old.

Dog Crates

I recommend people use plastic airline crates to house train dogs in. These plastic crates are easy to clean and can be taken outside and sprayed out when need be. When we house train puppies we keep our cleaning supplies right on top of the crate.

I used to recommend Kennel Aire Wire Dog crates. The problem with wire crates is they don't contain dog hair and even with a pan that goes into the crate they don't keep dirt inside the crate.

We don't put bedding in the crate. The only thing we would do is put in a piece of rubber cow mat. You will never hear your dog get up and turn around in the crate.

Housebreaking an Adult Dog Using the Umbilical Cord Method

Most puppies can be housebroken prior to 8 months of age using traditional methods. But for older dogs that are still having accidents in the house, the umbilical cord method should be used. This method has worked on the most difficult housebreaking cases and can be used with dogs of any age.

When the owner makes a commitment to success and is consistent with its application, the success rate using this method is very high.

Dogs do not eliminate in the house because of anger, spite, jealousy, boredom or mischief. With the exceptions of territorial urine marking, illness, or (rarely) separation distress syndrome, dogs go to the bathroom in the house for one reason: they have never been properly housetrained by the owner.

There are some common mistakes that owners make during early housebreaking attempts that can exacerbate the problem:

- the use of puppy pads inside the home
- too much freedom too soon
- punishment after the fact
- using the wrong cleaners to clean up the mess
- not using a dog crate

But even if the above mistakes have been made, Any Dog Can Be Housebroken!

Steps to take

1. Put a 6 foot leash on the dog and tie it to your belt. The dog is connected to you (umbilical cord). He goes where you go.
2. When it is not possible to keep the dog tethered to you on the leash, he should be placed in his crate. (Except for overnight, a dog should not be crated

for more than 3 to 4 consecutive hours. Many working people find it necessary to hire a pet sitter to give the dog an afternoon "break.")

3. Take the dog outside every hour using the verbal cue "want to go out?" in a happy high pitched tone when you get to the door. Do not wait for a "signal" from the dog - just take him out every hour, for about 5 minutes. Always USE THE SAME DOOR to exit.

4. Give the verbal cue "hurry up." If he eliminates outside, praise him in a happy, high pitched voice at the moment that he finishes doing his business.

5. Whenever the dog is not in his crate, he should be on the leash, attached to you. If he begins to urinate or defecate in your presence, correct him in a loud, low tone of voice. Don't scream and yell - you should startle, but not frighten the dog. Immediately take him outside and give the verbal cue "hurry up." If he eliminates outside, praise him in a happy, high pitched voice at the moment that he finishes doing his business.

6. After 10 consecutive days with no accidents, disconnect the leash and begin to allow limited freedom, using gates to confine the dog to one room of the house. BE SURE TO CONTINUE THE CONSTANT SUPERVISON at this stage! If you are not in the same room with the dog, put the dog in his crate. Be sure to keep an eye on the dog at all times. Continue this step for 30 days.

7. If there have been no accidents during the 30-day period in step 6, you can begin to allow a bit more freedom. Confine the dog to the initial room plus an adjoining room – do not give him freedom to roam throughout the entire house. You can begin to allow him to be alone in these 2 different rooms for very short periods of time. Be sure to crate him if you leave the house, even for a few minutes. Continue to take him out every hour, and continue to praise him when he goes to the bathroom outside. Continue this step for 30 days.

8. If there have been no accidents during the 30 day period in step 7, he can be now be given full run of

the house, but he should still be crated when you leave the house.

1. If your dog has an accident during step 6, 7 or 8, go back one step. If he has another accident after you back one step, go back to step 1 and start over again. Some dogs will need to be "connected" to you on the leash for a long period of time in order to become housebroken, so be patient. The good news is that once a dog had been housebroken using this method, he will usually not regress.

How to Train an Older Dog to Do New Tricks

While most people associate training with puppies, the reality is that dogs can learn at any age. Adult dogs are often easier to train than young puppies because they have more self-control. It's also important to keep training your dog as it matures. It will keep your dog's mind sharp and offer the mental stimulation and structure that it needs. While these tips are mainly for owners that have recently adopted an adult dog, they can also be used to train older pets that may need to gain new skills.

Be Patient

If you have just brought an adult dog into your home, allow him some time to adjust. An adult dog comes with its own history which can make it nervous about its new surroundings. Don't give up on your new dog after only a few days. Your adult dog may need a period of adjustment which can take anywhere from a few days to a month or so. Once your adult dog realizes it has found its forever home, it will soon settle into being part of the family. There may be some unique challenges and opportunities when it comes to training a shelter dog.

Use a Crate for Housetraining

Don't assume an adult dog is house trained or well-behaved in the house. Treat your adult dog just as you would a new puppy. Keep it in a crate when you are not able to supervise him. When you release it from the crate, take him immediately to the place outside where you want him to relieve himself. If it does not relieve itself, re-crate it and try again a little later.

Be sure that the crate you select is large enough and strong enough to contain your adult dog comfortably. The dog should be able to stand up, move around, and stretch out without difficulty. Soft-sided crates are often too flimsy to stand up to the needs of an adult dog; the best option is usually a metal wire crate that can be folded for transportation. Provide your crated dog with water, soft blankets, and chew toys, and be sure that you provide your pet with enough attention, exercise, and outdoor time to relieve itself.

If your adult dog is new to crates, introduce the concept slowly. Entice your dog to enter the crate by offering food, and keep it in the crate for only a few minutes at first. Avoid using the crate as a punishment or leaving your dog isolated in its crate for long periods.

The good news is that adult dogs have more control over their bladders and bowels than young puppies. The house training process usually goes much more quickly with adult dogs than with puppies or adolescent dogs who don't have this control yet.

Enroll in an Obedience Class

Your adult dog is perfectly capable of learning new things. Even if it has never had any obedience training in the past, your adult dog will benefit from learning basic commands, such as walking on a loose leash and lying down. An obedience class is a great place to work on this training.

An obedience class is also a great place for your adult dog to socialize with other dogs and people. It will allow you to see how it reacts to other dogs and strangers in a safe environment with a professional dog trainer on hand to offer advice.

Problems and Proofing

An adult dog may have been able to do things in its previous home that you don't want him to do in yours, such as jumping on guests or lying on the furniture. These tips will help ensure that your dog learns and retains appropriate behaviors for your home.

- Start teaching your adult dog the rules for your home as soon as possible.

- Consider teaching your dog self-control using the "Nothing in Life Is Free" (NILF) dog training method, which requires your dog to behave appropriately before getting the desired treat, walk, or positive attention.

- Be sure everyone is on the same page. It can be confusing to a dog when different members of the household have different standards of behavior, commands, or expectations. When everyone agrees on appropriate behaviors and uses the same commands and rewards, your dog will learn faster and retain its training longer.

Keep It Positive

Because you probably don't know for sure the type of experience your adult dog has had with training in the past, positive reinforcement methods are your best bet. Using tasty treats and plenty of praise are effective training methods for dogs of all ages and breeds. Keep things fun and upbeat rather than punishing your adult dog. This is a great way to strengthen the bond between you and your dog.

It may take some work at the beginning but teaching your adult dog basic commands and working on solving behavior problems from day one means your dog will soon settle into being a happy and healthy part of your family.

CHAPTER 9

How to Housebreak a Dog in 7 Days

If you have recently adopted a puppy, you are faced with the somewhat daunting challenge of housebreaking your new dog. While older dogs may require a bit more time and patience, a 3- to 6-month-old dog can be successfully housebroken in just seven days. For best results, you must follow the schedule to the letter, meaning you must remain at home all day with your new pup.

In order to housebreak your dog in as little as seven days, you must follow the schedule to the letter.

Once the first week is up, try to keep as much of the schedule as possible, taking the dog out and feeding at regular times. Praise and punishment are essential parts of housebreaking a dog; however, because a puppy's memory span lasts a maximum of 90 seconds, praise or punishment should occur as soon as the event passes. When the dog finishes going to the bathroom outside, give heavy verbal praise, using verbal punishment the instant you notice an accident occurring indoors.

How to Housebreak a Dog in Seven Days

Step 1:

Start each day by waking up at 7 a.m. and immediately taking the dog outside to go to the bathroom. Wait as long as necessary for the dog to go and then return to the house for playtime until 8 a.m. During playtime, the puppy can be allowed free time; however, it is best to give as much attention to your new dog as possible.

Step 2:

Give your new dog something to eat and drink at 8 a.m., after a good play session. Watch the dog carefully after he eats, as some dogs will have the urge to go to the bathroom immediately after eating. If your dog shows signs of need, such as sniffing or wandering to hidden areas in the house, pick him up and go directly outside. Whenever possible, wait a full half hour, until 8:30 a.m., to go outside for potty time.

Step 3:

Allow your puppy to play freely in a small, closed room, such as the kitchen. It is best to keep the puppy in your sight during free time so that you can quickly notice signs of bathroom needs. If you are crate training your puppy while housebreaking, place the dog in her crate from 9:30 a.m. to 12:30 p.m. Remember to place toys and chewies in the crate for entertainment; however, no food or water.

Step 4:

Release the puppy from the crate or end free time at 12:30 p.m., giving the dog food and water. Again, wait up to half an hour if possible and then take the dog outside. After returning inside, give the dog at least 30 minutes of free time to play before placing him in the crate if you so choose.

Step 5:

Feed the dog for the third and final time at 6 p.m., taking her outside within half an hour. This is a good time to take the puppy for a walk or play outside so that she can explore the world a bit. After at least 30 minutes of outdoor or play time, you can place her in the crate if you wish.

Step 6:

Offer the puppy water at 8 p.m.; however, after 8:15 p.m. the dog should not drink any more water to help to make it through the night. Take the dog out within 30 minutes after he drinks. Follow up with some play time and time in the crate, if desired. Take the dog out before bed at 11 p.m., keeping him in a crate overnight to prevent accidents.

CHAPTER 10

Housebreaking Your Puppy: Do's And Don'ts

The process of housebreaking often brings on feelings of nervousness and worry, but the process does not have to be stressful—for you or the puppy.

The truth is this is a situation in which you have Mother Nature working with you right from the start while puppy training. When the puppies are first born, they eat and they relieve themselves inside the den, but the mother always cleans them. There is never a scent of urine or feces where the puppies eat, sleep, and live. When they get old enough, they learn to use outside areas as they imitate their mother.

Conditioning

In this way, all dogs become conditioned never to eliminate in their dens. From two to four months of age, most pups pick up on the concept of housebreaking and crate training quite easily since it is part of their natural programming.

Puppy's Digestive Tract

Another built-in plus when it comes to housebreaking is our puppy's digestive tract, which is extremely quick and efficient. Five to 30 minutes after the puppy eats, she'll want to defecate. So, with a consistent eating schedule, and your attention to the clock, your puppy can maintain regular trips outside.

In the early days of housebreaking, you also want to make sure the puppy has a place to relieve herself where she feels safe; a place that seems and smells familiar. Have you noticed how dogs will often eliminate in the very same spot they've done so before? The scent acts like a trigger.

Your Energy

As always, remember that your own energy is a big factor in your housebreaking efforts. If you are feeling nervous or impatient or are trying to rush a puppy to relieve herself, that can also stress her out. Using a loud, high squeaky tone to encourage your puppy to "go potty" is a distraction to the dog, so try and avoid any conversation at all.

Setting a Routine

First thing every morning, bring your puppy outside to the same general area. It is important to remain consistent throughout the process so your puppy can learn the habit.

Once your puppy has successfully gone outside, it is important to reward the good behavior. It doesn't have to be a big, loud celebration, but a simple quiet approval or a treat can get the message across of a job well done.

Positive Reinforcement

Don't punish your puppy for an accident or do anything to create a negative association with her bodily functions. Stay calm and assertive and quietly remove the puppy to the place where you want him to go.

Done correctly, housebreaking should not be a turbulent production but just a matter of putting a little extra work into getting your puppy on a schedule during the first weeks after she arrives at your home. Don't let unnecessary stress over this very natural, uncomplicated process taint any of the joy surrounding the puppy training process and your new dog's puppyhood.

CHAPTER 11

How To Housebreak a Puppy: Tips from Experts

Learning how to housebreak a puppy is a huge part of the job of raising your puppy and requires a lot of patience and consistency.

Some dogs can learn quickly, but other puppies could take months to potty train. So, you'll probably have a trial-and-error period in which you have to try different things to determine what works for you, your puppy and your family.

While some accidents are inevitable, here are some tips from experts for housebreaking, or potty training, and training your puppy.

Housebreaking Your Puppy

- "Take your puppy outside about 15 minutes after every meal. At this point, they should be "ready to go" – plus, it's just a really great habit for them to get into!"
- "Take your dog outside to potty at the same place each time. Your dog will learn to potty train much quicker".

Housebreaking a Puppy With a Crate

- "Do start leaving the puppy by itself in the crate right away. Even if it's only for 10 or fifteen minutes, puppies need to learn that their family will always come back."
- "When puppies are crate-trained, they'll avoid soiling inside it, leading to an easier time to teach them to go to the bathroom somewhere else."

- "To get puppies to love their crates, they should be 'where the action is' in the house-- they should eat in their crates, and the crate should be available (open) for naps. A very special treat, like a frozen Kong stuffed with a mixture of yogurt and treats, should be given in the crate when the family leaves the house."

Teaching Your Puppy Commands

- "You have to start this as early as possible. It can begin in the home, and all you need are loads of treats and to tell them to 'come' whenever they are away from you. They will learn to associate the command with the reward and will pick it up quickly. Once you get outside walking, this is one of the most valuable commands to have."

- "Use small words. When you want your puppy not to do something, use one word such as "No" or "Come" or "Stay." These small words are easier for your dog to remember.:

- "It's far better to train your puppy regularly in short bursts, such as on a daily basis, vs trying to cram in everything in over a few hours."

- "To begin teaching a sit behavior, get on your dog's level, hold a treat close to his or her nose and slowly make an arch shape with your hand. As his head follows the treat, his or her butt will lower to the ground. As soon as his or her butt hits the ground, reward your pup with the treat."

- "On some occasions, your dog might just not 'get it,' or you might feel very impatient, so just skip this session and play a good ol' catch instead!"

- "A lot of people stop giving their puppy and dog treats once they have fully learned a command. Then, they wonder why their dog has started listening a little less (or not at all). Dogs love rewards. You don't have to give a treat every time when they are fully trained, but maybe every other time or every two times so that they know there is still something in it for them."

- "Train at any public location you can think of - from parks over outdoor malls to the city center - as often as possible (once your puppy has received all his shots). Many dogs don't focus in public because they are rarely trained in busy places."

- "All super-engineered tricks you see on Instagram have started with a very basic command and reward upon execution. Training a dog takes time. Trying to go too quickly will get your dog overwhelmed and you frustrated."

-

What Not to Do When House Training Your Puppy

- "You see a lot of advice about sticking a dog's nose in their mess, yelling at them, or even giving their backsides a smack. None of this will help with house training, and it might actually make things worse because of the negative attention. Take them outside regularly; reward them with treats and ALL the praise when they go outside. When it happens inside, ignore it completely and act like nothing happened."

- "The worst thing a trainer can do is get frustrated or aggravated at their dog. If you instead make it fun and engaging, your dog will love to get trained, look forward to it, be more dependable, and feel more at home."

The puppy stage is full of excitement and rewards, both for the puppy and for the owner! At the same time, there will certainly be periods of frustration through the housebreaking process. As many of our puppy training experts pointed out, make sure not to put too much pressure on yourself or your puppy to be perfect. It's a learning process for both of you, and that means there might be some bumps and stumbles along the way!

With these tips, you should have the knowledge you need to start your relationship with your puppy on the right foot!

7 Trainer-Approved Puppy Housebreaking Tips

We're bringing home a new puppy. Do you have any suggestions for house training?

Patience is key when it comes to housebreaking because every pup will pick up the process at his own pace. And unless a dog is taught where to eliminate, he'll look for any spot that's convenient and safe, which often ends up being the carpeting! Unfortunately, dogs aren't born with the moral reasoning to understand that going to the bathroom inside the house is wrong.

Since dogs innately want to keep their personal area clean, they will venture away from their own territory to use the bathroom. But many owners make the mistake of giving a puppy too much space too fast. In this case, the dog has little incentive to wait to go outside, since his personal roaming space only makes up a small portion of the home.

Tip #1: Get a Crate

It's best to use confinement to teach your dog that he has to wait to go to the bathroom outside the house. You can do this by purchasing a crate, so the puppy has just enough space to turn around and lie down. Another alternative, if possible, is to keep the puppy by your side at all times while clipped to a four- to six-foot leash.

Tip #2: Honor the 15-Minute Rule

Puppies are most likely to use the bathroom within 15 minutes of eating, drinking, playing, exercising or waking up from a nap. After any of these activities, your puppy should be given an opportunity to go to the bathroom.

A general rule of thumb for how long puppies can hold their bladders: one hour for every month of age, plus one. So if a puppy is two months old, he can wait up to three hours. However, this varies from dog to dog, and a puppy should be taken out more often than his maximum hold time. I train owners to take puppies out to the bathroom every one to two hours or after any activity that stimulates elimination.

It's important to consult your veterinarian if your puppy seems to have difficulty holding his elimination for reasonable amounts of time for his age, because this could signal a medical problem.

Tip #3: Reward a Job Well Done

When it's time for a bathroom break, take your puppy outside to the same proper elimination area each time. If he goes to the bathroom within five minutes, praise him and offer treats as soon as he does his business.

Don't take your puppy immediately back to his confinement area, which can actually read as punishment to him. Instead, opt for a 10-minute block of supervised play in a bigger area before putting him back in the confined space. However, if your puppy does not eliminate outside, calmly place him back in his confinement area, wait 15 minutes and then try again outdoors.

Tip #4: Accidents Happen

Never punish your puppy if he has an accident in the house. This only teaches the dog to fear the idea of going to the bathroom when people are around, and he will likely still go in the house — just not when his owner is looking. Instead, if you catch your puppy in the act, you can interrupt him with an "oops," and immediately take him to his proper elimination area outside.

Consider using enzymatic cleaners on any potty spots to keep your dog from smelling previous accidents and going there again.

Tip #5: Introduce Space Gradually

As your puppy stays accident-free in the confined area, you can gradually expand his space privileges by introducing him to a new room. After one week of success without accidents, open up yet another area of your home.

However, if accidents start happening, confine him back to the previous level of success. And keep to his regular schedule of bathroom breaks, rewarding for proper elimination, throughout the entire training process.

Tip #6: Get Out of Bed

During the night, you may need to take your puppy outside multiple times. Don't push your puppy to hold his bladder past the limit for his age or individual ability. If accidents happen at night, it's critical that you take him out more often — the more a dog messes in his personal space, the more comfortable he will become with lying in his filth, making housebreaking difficult.

Tip #7: Don't Rely on Puppy Pads and Newspaper

Although dogs can be transitioned away from them, it makes the house-training process more complicated. I often see canines who are trained to go on pads as puppies, but they're not allowed to do so as adults, which only leads to confusion and accidents in the home.

CHAPTER 12

How to Housebreak a Puppy If You Work All Day

Puppies are a sweet and often irresistible addition to a household. But, like all babies, they need to be trained to use the bathroom properly, and in the correct place. While being at work for hours makes the process difficult, consistency is the key to training your new pup.

Step 1

Create a small, gated area -- approximately three feet by five feet -- where the puppy can be confined. This can also be a crate. The floor should be covered with something that is safe from accidents, such as vinyl in the kitchen. The puppy will not want to soil his living area, so keeping it small will help discourage accidents.

Step 2

Cover the floor with several layers of newspapers to contain any accidents the puppy has during the day while you are at work. If he does have an accident on these -- and if he is by himself for more than a few hours, it needs to be expected -- take them to his bathroom spot; the smell will help him associate that this is where he is supposed to eliminate.

Step 3

Place a soft bed in one corner of this area for the puppy to sleep in; it should be made of fabric that can be easily washed and dried.

Step 4

Begin an immediate routine with the new puppy to avoid accidents. Feed him, walk him and play with him on a regular schedule around your job. Assume that he can only hold his bladder for one hour multiplied by his age; so at two months, he will need to go outside every two hours.

Step 5

Pick a spot that will be the puppy's bathroom and take him to it every two hours, on his leash, when you are home with him especially after he eats, drinks or wakes up.

Step 6

Do not yell at the puppy if you catch him going to the bathroom in his confined area; instead, firmly say "No", take him outside to his bathroom area, and praise him when he finishes going there. Allow him to play outside with you for a few minutes so that he associates going outside with also getting to play; this can help him avoid going on the floor.

Step 7

Watch your puppy closely when you are home with him for any sign that he needs to go outside; this could include pacing, scratching at the door or whining. Immediately take him outside and praise him when he uses the proper bathroom spot.

Step 8

Avoid feeding your puppy right before you leave for work; he will usually need to use the bathroom within an hour of eating.

CHAPTER 13

Housebreaking Your Puppy Without Losing Your Mind

There are lots of things to look forward to when adopting a puppy: cuddling, playtime, kisses, and the pitter-patter those four tiny little feet. One thing that dog owners do not look forward to, however, is housebreaking their new puppy. A notoriously challenging task that can try your patience and lead to some embarrassing moments, housebreaking is a necessary part of puppyhood.

Here are some advices I can mention on successfully train your puppy to "go outside." Trust me, we've been through it all with our dogs, so I understand!

Based on my experience and what I've learnt from dog trainers around the country, we believe that there are three universal rules of housebreaking your puppy:

Consistency

Dogs thrive on routine, especially when they are young. Housebreaking is no exception. The "Dog Whisperer" himself, Cesar Millan, asserts that daily consistency is the key to successfully housebreaking your dog.

Even before you bring your puppy home for the first time, work with your family to a devise a daily dog schedule. Meals, walks, playtime, sleep, trips outside – try work in these activities at the same time every day. Your puppy will soon learn to associate these times with these activities. "7:00AM, I eat. 7:30AM, I go outside. 8:00AM, I play with toys…"

When creating this schedule, be sure to include plenty of "potty breaks," and not just first thing in the morning and before bed. A good rule of thumb from the Humane Society of the United States: a puppy can typically control his bladder for one hour for every month of age. Because of this fact, Millan suggests scheduling "potty breaks" at various times throughout the day, including immediately following each meal, after waking up from a nap and after long play sessions.

Finally, be aware and vigilant about where your puppy spends his time in your home. Set clear rules about what rooms are off-limits to the puppy, and make sure everyone (even the kids and visitors), follows them. You can use baby gates to help enforce these rules, or you can talk to your DogWatch dealer about indoor hidden boundary solutions. These safe, small, wireless systems will teach your dog to recognize "off-limits" areas, such as formal rooms, kitchen counters, couches and even the cat litter box.

I know it will be challenging to fit a rigid schedule into your fast-paced, crowded, multi-tasking life. Just remember: establishing a routine and sticking to it is the fastest way to rid your house of puppy "accidents."

Commitment

Neglecting the routine, on the other hand, can quickly lead to housebreaking failures and months of frustration. This brings us to the second rule of housebreaking – be committed. Teaching your dog important lessons like housebreaking when they are young is a great way to set up your pet for a healthy, well-behaved future.

Of course, commitment means that even if you hate getting up at, say 7:00AM on Saturday morning, you'll have to tough it out. If this strict schedule is a struggle for you, ask family or friends to help, reminding them that help now makes everyone's life easier later. And don't forget, when you're walking on those dreary early Saturdays, you can always take a nap with your new cuddle buddy when you get home, once all the hard work is done!

Another aspect of this commitment is promptly cleaning up after your dog when he has an accident in the home. A dog can quickly associate an area of the house as fair game if he can still smell the scent of his waste there. Keep a supply of pet cleaner in the house at all times, and thoroughly clean messes as soon as you spot them. Your dog will appreciate it, and so will you, once that odor disappears.

Maintain this vigilance by keeping a close watch on your puppy at all times, encouraging and rewarding good behavior. When your dog does his "business" outside, reward her immediately. If you happen to catch her eliminating inside, interrupt her and firmly address her with "outside" or any other chosen word or phrase you associate with housebreaking.

If, however, you catch it after the fact, do not scold your puppy and definitely don't rub his nose it in. Experts agree that this tactic will only serve to make your dog afraid to eliminate in front of you, and encourage her to eliminate in hidden places when you are not looking.

In addition, to the added cleaning time, this negative reinforcement actually prolongs the entire housebreaking process and can lead to more training problems down the road.

Finally, for those times when you are unable to watch over your puppy, keep him in a crate or another enclosed area. This will not only protect him from common household hazards (e.g. falling objects, poisonous plants or food, open windows, etc.), but also teach him how to be alone, thus preventing separation anxiety – another behavior challenge that leads to household messes.

Patience

This last rule of housebreaking is, surprisingly, the most difficult to follow. We all love our puppies, but even the most dedicated pet parent can reach the breaking point when they are forced to deal with yet another carpet stain or morning mess. How will you get through it?

First of all, acknowledge the fact that, just like humans, no dog is perfect. Sure, you may envy your neighbor's well-training pooch and spot-free couch, but remember, they had to go through the same process as you are going through now with your puppy. Some dogs may be housebroken in a matter of weeks, while others might need a few months before they start to catch on. (Chihuahua owners especially know what it feels like to fall into the latter category!) If your dog is struggling, stay focused on the routine – you'll get there eventually. Meanwhile, remind yourself about the other tasks that your dog is doing well – perhaps he gets along great with the house cat, or he doesn't pull on the leash as much as he used to. Every dog is unique – that's what makes them so special!